www.tredition.de

AF198288

Willi Wendland

Back Pain
„Bye Bye"

A booklet on health,

pain-free without medication

© 2019 Willi Wendland

© Illustrations & pictures: Willi Wendland

Publishing house und Print:
tredition GmbH, Halenreie 40-44, 22359 Hamburg, Germany

ISBN
Paperback: 978-3-7497-0631-0
Hardcover: 978-3-7497-0632-7
e-Book: 978-3-7497-0633-4

About the Author

Willi Wendland, born on 19-08-1950 in East Westphalia, Germany.

I don't make any healing promises, I only report about my long lasting experience with SMT® "Gentle Manual Therapy" according to Dr. Michael Graulich.

From my own experience, I can say how SMT® "Gentle Manual Therapy" affects the whole body. Already after the first two exercises, I had almost no pain anymore. The two exercises are the basis to become or to stay painless without medication.

You can find SMT® Wendland under:

https://www.smt-wendland.de/

My story

Back pain has been a constant theme even during my youth. I learned the profession of a butcher. My back pain increased due to the hard work and standing at the table processing the meat.

A few years after the apprenticeship, I was no longer able to do my job, even though I did sport (running, strength training) every day. Despite muscle build-up, I could not ge the back pain under control.

On the advice of the job center, I learned the profession of a technical draughtman in mechanical engineering and later office clerk.

But my back pain kept coming back. Through daily training, running, strength training and tablets, I was able to do some of my work as an office clerk.

I was responsible for order picking in the paint-chemical warehouse and in sales. One morning I was supposed to bring two containers of acid, each weighing 65 kg, to the sales department, but I never arrived there.

I could just lift one of the containers onto a car, but I already noticed a strong pain in my back. When I wanted to put the second container on the car as well, it was impossible. All of a sudden I was all crooked and could not move anymore.

The pain was almost unbearable, the sweat was on my forehead, tears were running down my face:

The sciatic nerve was pinched somehow.

I had to go to the hospital, got two injections, but I remained all crooked. The pain could be alleviated a little.

An **"odyssey"** began, from one orthopedist to the next. First, I had to get into the MRI. There I was diagnosed with two herniated discs L4/L5 prolapse and L3/L4 a pre-curvature. The diagnosis brought me to the Paracelsus Clinic in Osnabrück for 6 weeks. At the clinic, they still suspected polio, because I was not getting straight, despite daily infusions and tablets. I was punctured, but fortunately, polio was ruled out.

After about 6 weeks I left the hospital. They couldn't help me there, but at the final consultation, the doctor told me that I should build up certain muscles with sport. In physiotherapy, they would know how to do that. My family doctor would get a special report and write down the muscle-building therapies for me. There I was with two herniated discs and no improvement.

It started all over again, only I became more and more depressed. I even went to a neurologist several times and had my nerve tracts measured, because nobody could really help me. Life was just grey. After about half a year I came to an orthopaedist in Herford.

He should decide once again whether a surgery would be appropriate after all. He said, "We want to try again infusions and injections between the vertebrae under the CT."

After the therapy, I still wasn't exactly straight. But the orthopaedist suggested a cure first. That's how I came to Bad Sassensdorf. Two days after my arrival a place at the breakfast table next to me became free. There someone sat down next to me, named Peter.

And as usual, you tell what kind of problems you have. Peter's right hip (acetabulum and femoral head) was eaten up by a hip dysplasia. The X-rays exactly showed that. Bone parts were already missing in the acetabulum, and the femoral head did not look good either.

Peter has no new hip until today

He said to me that he has no problems and no pain with it, because he always corrects his hip and the sacrum. I asked for hip and sacrum corrections, what does that mean?

He explained me the SMT® which he had learned from Dr. Michael Graulich. Since that time he did not have any pain because of his daily exercises. I couldn't believe that something like that was possible. I thought I had already gone through all the therapies, but none could help me to get a straight back again. The pain was only bearable with medication.

When I told him my story about the two herniated discs, Peter said to me, "Oh, you know, your problems have nothing to do with the herniated discs, but only with your muscles in your buttocks.

The tension in the buttocks, which spreads upwards, causes herniated discs. This is caused by muscles called Piriformis and Obturatorius."

I looked at him and no longer understood the world.

Then he told me why the two muscles in our buttocks are responsible.

They are attached to the outside of the trochanter and inside of the sacrum. There the sciatic nerve runs through and gets jammed. Because the hip slips out again and again and there is no pressure from the side in daily life that can bring back the hip into the acetabulum, muscle build-up first brings relief. In the long run, the tension increases and the back pain worsens. Herniated discs are only caused by the tense muscles in the buttocks, which run upwards into the back.

It was quite plausible what he said, but I couldn't believe it. He said,: "No problem. If you want to become straight and painless again, I can show you the two exercises which I frequently do every day."

I was very skeptical, a patient to help me?

I wanted to discard this possibility, but he said, "Willi, I have with me a book by Dr. Michael Graulich. If you want to read it, I'll give it to you. 'Miracles take a little longer' is the title of the book."

After having read the book for one day, I was very curious what next I had to face. After breakfast, I asked Peter if he could show me the two exercises. No sooner said than done. In his room he said to me, "Lay down on my bed." Peter had explained to me before what he would do. I had to leave my shoes on, so that he could see how different my leg length were.

I was laying on the bed, and Peter pressed my heels back with his thumbs lifting my legs. He said, "Look at that, the difference in leg length." I couldn't believe it, the difference was about 5-6 cm. He said, "That's your problem. We are all born with legs of the same length, but in the course of life the hip shifts due to daily sitting, crossing the legs, bending under 90degrees, squatting, driving the car, etc." I couldn't believe what Peter told me. "Then all the people have the same problems," I said. "Yeah, but nobody tells you that. Of course, the doctors know this, but they don't have time for the patient. Only about 3 to 5 minutes, I guess. So, again and again, painkillers are administered in form of pills or injections and muscle building proposed. That is easier. However, it is the wrong approach, the wrong way, because the real problem is not solved. As I have already said, the reason why we get all this foot-, knee-, back-, hip-, shoulder-pain, and headache is always 99 % due to the muscles in the buttocks.

Through the muscles Piriformis and Obturatorius, the sciatic nerve runs and gets pinched. As a result, the muscles become tight, the nerves become even more pinched and the tension in the buttocks increases.

The pull of the muscles continues upwards or downwards into the legs. The musculature and the resulting displacement of all joints are mostly responsible for the pain throughout the body.

So I was quite astonished. But actually quite logical, only that so far no therapist or doctor told me that.

Peter put my legs back on the bed and said, "The left leg was longer, so you start with the right leg and end with the left."

I asked, "How to start. What do you mean by that ?" "You bend your leg 90 degrees and press against your thigh. When the leg is lowered, the pressure helps the hip to get back into the correct position. This also causes the two muscles Piriformis and Obturatorius to get the correct length, so that the sciatic nerve will no more be pinched. Always alternating right, left, etc. You have to do this exercise 4 times a day in bed and 4 times in the evening, and during the day as often as possible, I'll still explain it to you. You can also do this in an upright position, but the exercises in bed should be done daily."

SMT® „Soft Manual Therapy"

In the years from 2003 to 2011, I learned the SMT® „Soft Manual Therapy" in several seminars with Dr. Michael Graulich.

Dr. Michael Graulich is a specialist in general medicine from Ottobeuren in the Allgäu region. Years ago he learned the basic termes of SMT® Soft Manual Therapy according to Dorn and developed them further. So he integrated the Chinese medicine, the meridians, and the functional circle theory into the Dorn method.

Likewise he integrated the knowledge of osteopaths, so that after a few years Dr. Michael Graulich named this work also SMT® Soft Manual Therapy after Dr. Michael Graulich.

I have been helping people with back pain for many years with this therapy after Graulich.

According to my point of view, the two exercises from SMT® are the most important exercises to become or remain pain-free, and everyone can use them very easily.

I'll explain the first exercise

Hip and leg length correction

Raise the right leg 90 degrees until the thigh is almost horizontal.

Now press your fist against the thigh, directly on the outside, as shown in the pictures.

Move your leg slightly outwards. Now put again the leg on the floor next to the other one, so that the foot describes a small arc, just like when riding a bicycle, until it stands next to the other foot again.

Now lift your left leg 90 degrees and press your first against the thigh. When the leg is lowered again, turn it slightly outwards and place it next to the other foot again.

This exercise is particularly recommended before and after any sport, cycling, driving a car or after sitting for long periods, desc working, etc. In stubborn cases, it should be performed after each sitting.

In my opinion, this is the most important exercise for everyone to become or stay healthy.

I do this about 100 times daily.

Our hip is pushed or pulled out every day in many everyday situations. With this exercise we can bring it back into the right position in order to put the Piriformis and Obturatorius muscles back to their normal length.

The human problem

We don't have a muscle in the buttocks that can pull the hip back where it belongs to.

In everyday life, there is also no external pressure that corrects the hip again. With this exercise, we can support the hip to take its optimal seat again.

We can see the importance of always bringing the hip back again in the animals. For example, on the dogs. A dog gets up and simply stretches. One foot backward and then the other foot backward and then both front feet to the front.

Horses stand up first with the front feet and then with the hind feet. Cows the other way, first with the hind legs and then with the front legs.

This gives the animals a possibility to correct the sacrum, whereby the musculature is loosened and the spinal column becomes straight.

Whenever the spine is straight, you can't get sick. In general, animals are not sick.

This means that if our spine is straight and without tension, we will also become healthy and painfree. That is just logical.

Human beings do not have these possibilities like animals. Probably they got lost in the course of evolution through our upright position. With the SMT®, we have found a method to make this correction by means of two exercises.

I don't promise that you will be able to get rid of your pain right away by doing the hip and sacrum correction once, but if you do these exercises regularly every day, you will feel better from day to day. I experienced it on my own body.

Your commitment and some patience are the most important things you need. You only can do that!

I can only tell you how I do it every day for myself and together with my wife.

„Success is in having exactly the skills you need right now."
(Quote: Henry Ford)

Many people have asked me why I don't pass on my knowledge, write it down or publish it in the media. They believe that all people are interested in such and other exercises, which will realign our bodies and make them free of pain.

Explanation

Each vertebral segment contains 4 nerves supplying all organs: the heart, kidneys, liver, stomach, muscles, skin, etc.

If this is no longer possible due to the pulling of the muscles Piriformis / Obturatorius, the tension in the buttocks increases and the sciatic nerve becomes trapped. The tension continues in the back.

Our muscular system looks like a spiral. It stretches and turns the vertebrae sometimes to the right and sometimes to the left. When this happens, the muscles pinch the nerves in the vertebrae and the organs are no longer properly supplied.

One day the organ fails because the supply no longer functions, so that the person becomes ill.
We get back pain or other diseases.

The reason is simple:

The hip, which, again and again, is slipping out or is getting pulled out in many positions, cannot return to its original position on its own and the tension becomes stronger and stronger in the buttocks and the back. I can only tell you about myself.

I have no back pain any more since I have made this correction every day. I can do all the work, whether standing for a long time, sitting, lifting heavily, bending down, laying on the floor and getting up again. A few years ago, I was no longer able to do all this anymore.

As described, I am now correcting my hip about 100 times a day; the exercise takes little time.
A dog or any other animal does not ask, should I stretch or get up in a different way? No, they just do it! Only human beings don't, and why not?
No one says why there is pain and how to get rid of it.

NOW you have the opportunity to start, because this is the beginning to become painless again.

Excerpt from the book

„Wunder dauern etwas länger" - Wonders take a little longer

by Dr. Michael Graulich. Margarethen Publishing House, Ottobeuren, Germany. First German edition, 1996.
4th revised edition 2009, page 142 following

The Muscles

Erection and maintaining an upright posture of the spinal column

3.2.6.1 Physical-anatomical correlations for the erection and maintaining an upright posture of the spinal column
Before I discuss scolioses, hyper-kyphosis, and hyper-lordosis from SMT®, I have to deal with erection and maintaining the upright posture of the human being.

One can only be surprised that science that regards itself as a natural science claims such nonsense on these topics. The doctrine of classical medicine on this subject is simplified but succinct:

That the musculature of people with changes or complaints of the spinal column is too weak to keep the spine straight. To straighten the spine and to heal the complaints, you have to train and strengthen these muscles through sport and gymnastics, i.e. to build up muscles.

The doctrine of classical medicine, that the musculature holds the human being upright and straight, is as wrong as the statement that the Earth is a disc.

How can erection and upright posture really be explained if the static-physical laws and anatomical conditions are put into the right context?

For the statics of any upright object, the condition of the basis is of primary and fundamental importance.

For a building, this means that if the foundation is sloping, the top of the building will crack and the cracks will spread downwards in the process of time. This is because,if the foundation is sloping, the degree of the deviation from the vertical at the top of a building is many times greater than in the lower sections of the building.

Of course, deviations above have static effects below, but these are secondary.

Which physical forces and anatomical facts play a role in the erection of the human body and its upright posture from a static point of view?.
1. *The base of the spine is the upper edge of the sacrum and thus the pelvis.*
2. *If the base becomes crooked, the spine on which it is resting and straightening up also becomes crooked.*
3. *The back musculature extends in three layers arranged one upon the other from bottom to top.*
4. *The back muscles are attached to the vertebrae and the neighboring ribs.*

5. *Due to the vertical course of the back muscles from bottom to top, they develop a traction force for physical-anatomical reasons.*

6. *By means of this traction force, the human being is straightened up, namely by the fact that the back-musculature pulls the human being up (from the quadruped stand) high into the vertical at the back.*

7. *The musculature belongs to the musculoskeletal system and has high elasticity because it has to stretch and contract again during muscular work.*

8. *It is impossible to generate static stability by an external elastic system. One would never try to fasten an erected pole with rubber bands because it is clear to everyone that the bands would give way and the pole would fall.*

9. *The assertion that the musculature keeps the person upright and straight is, therefore, wrong, because it is not able to do so due to its elasticity. On the contrary, when the traction force generated by the back muscles increases, the spine gives way and becomes crooked.*

10. *The upright posture is a function of the spine, therefore our skeletal system is also called the holding apparatus.*

11. *The physical force of the upright posture is a pressure force dissipation, created by the weight of the upper body and the head, which occurs primarily via the vertically arranged and mutually supporting vertebral joints (facets) and secondarily via the vertebral bodies stacked one on top of the other.*

12. A problem-free pressure force dissipation is only secured, if the spinal column has its physiological swings forward and backward, but is not bent sideways, but straight. This means that the vertebral joints (facets) must not deviate laterally from the vertical, otherwise, they lose their holding function.
13. In this function, the traction force of the back muscles in particular, but also the abdominal muscles, must not become too high (the back muscles attach themselves to the spine), because a too high traction force causes the spine to give way and becomes scoliotic, hyper-kyphotic and hyper-lordotic. At the same time, the vertebrae tilt in the rotational position, causing scoliosis to a segment.
14. Through the interaction of traction force through physiological tension (erection) in the back musculature and the dissipation of pressure force via the bony spine (upright posture), man can remain upright.

The summary of these 14 physical-anatomical laws is:

a) That the human pelvis must be absolutely straight

b) That there must not be more tension in the back muscles than the physiologically necessary basic tension (basic tone), which is different for each person depending on size and weight.

c) That the bony spine must be straight to keep the person upright. It must not be scoliotic, hyper-kyphotic or hyper-lordotic.

3.2.6.2 Various causes of increased tension in the back muscles

At the beginning of this chapter, I should discuss another physiological basic law, which in this form, according to my knowledge, has never been defined in such a way:

When a nerve is irritated (whether it is a mechanical, thermal or chemical irritation), the muscles, tendons, and ligaments which are supplied by this nerve are getting tensed up.
The muscle tensions caused by damaged nerves can develop into spasticity.

As long as there is tension or spasticity, the nerve is more or less severely damaged, but it is still alive.

A dead nerve develops a flaccid paralysis.

The biggest problem of all people is that in the course of life more and more tension develops in the entire body musculature.

In the course of the aging process the basic tone, i. e. the basic tension in the entire body musculature (cross-striped and smooth) increases. This increase in tension occurs at different speeds and to different degrees in people.

I regard this process as the actual expression of aging. I cannot explain how and what causes an increase in the basic muscular tension, and I leave this to the scientists who deal with aging processes and their backgrounds.

The result is that:

with increasing age, more and more effort is required to avoid behavior that damages the joints and spine and/ or a greater therapeutic effort to restore order to the joints and spine.

Psychological stress increases the tension in the striated but also plain musculature. In this mechanism, the background can be seen that many physicians see a strained or disturbed psyche as the cause of pain syndromes, but also of other diseases. This doctrine is wrong. A sick psyche aggravates pain and other illnesses but is not their actual cause.

There is no psychologically induced disease without organic findings. Not knowing the primary and fundamental cause of a disease or pain does not justify the claim that it does not exist.

The general cause of pain and disease can always be found in the findings caused by damage to joints and spine due to nerve entrapment.

Even if a psychological trauma can be identified as the cause of pain or illness, these ailments are caused by an increase in tension in the body musculature caused by psychological trauma.

As a result, damages to joints and spine increase, resulting in nerve entrapment or worsening.

This process, in turn, leads to pain syndromes and diseases.

No herb has grown against getting older, even if society likes to pay homage to the anti-aging god. "Don't worry be happy" doesn't work either in everyday life as we humans would like it. But it is possible for every human being to keep his joints and spine in good order or to restore them after damage.

With SMT® people have a means in their hands to prevent and/or cure diseases.

Hence, man is not helplessly at the mercy of his fate.

I thank Dr. Michael Graulich for allowing me to learn the SMT. I was able to help many people with back pain, with my information and showing them the exercises.

We can help ourselves, but we have to start. Everyone can do these two exercises with two arms and two legs.

This booklet will help you to do them daily and to correct the hip and the sacrum. The more often you perform these exercises, the less pain you will experience and the better you will be able to move.

I cannot make any healing promises, I have been pain-free for years and have been able to help many people with my information.

First of all, it is important to bring the muscles Piriformin and Obtuatorius back to the level which they originally had, so that the muscles in the buttocks can loosen again. The buttocks are **one of the most important parts of the body** that we have, it must always be loose, because a tense muscle cannot work properly.

Everyone knows that when the neck muscles are tense, you can't move your head properly. A relaxed, loose muscle is optimum.

The first exercise helps to loosen the muscles.

Lift one leg, slightly turn 90 degrees to the side, now press one leg against the thigh as described in the pictures and after a small outward movement return the leg downwards next to the foot. The same is done with the other leg, slightly turn 90 degrees to the side, press against the thigh and put down the leg as described. This exercise should be done several times a day because it relaxes.

Lying on the back:

This exercise can be done in a lying position. It is important that you do the exercise in bed in the evening so that the two muscles Piriformis and Obturatorius can relax. The exercise should also be done in the morning in bed. In the morning it is most important because you turn around at night and your hips are pushed out. It may result in tension. But if you do the exercise 4-5 times in bed in the evening and in the morning, you can remove some of the tension.

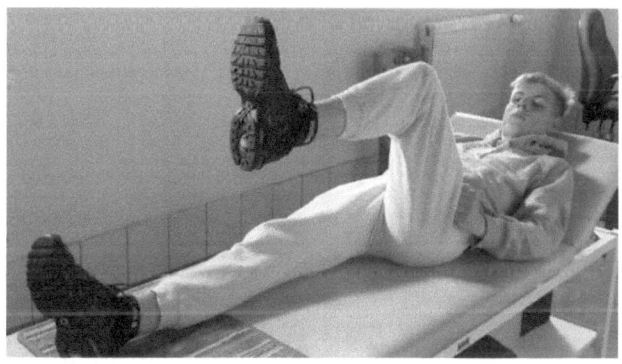

The procedure is the same as in standing position. You bend one leg 90 dgrees until the thigh and torso form a right angle. You put your fist against the thigh as shown in the picture, but only when the leg is lowered again (fist against the trouser seam, keep arms as long as they are) you press against the thigh, while at the same time you put the leg down with a slight bow movement. Make sure that you press with your fist against your thigh until the exercise leg is next to the other one.

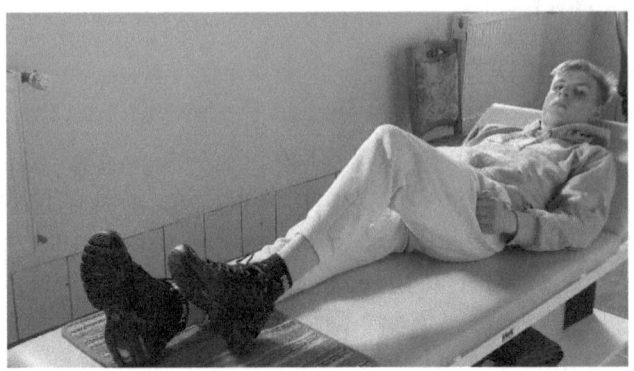

This exercise is particularly efficient, if carried out daily in bed before going to sleep, because the femoral head is then in the hip socket throughout the night and the ligaments can regenerate.

This efficiency is also achieved in the morning before getting up. If the exercise is done regularly 4-5 times in bed, you can get up painlessly after a short time.

The exercises in bed do not relieve you from further daily exercises, they only help you to release the tension in your body.

The second exercise

The correction of the sacrum is actually a little more difficult. But the most effective solution is to work with a tennis or a rubber ball on a door frame.

Like in the pictures.

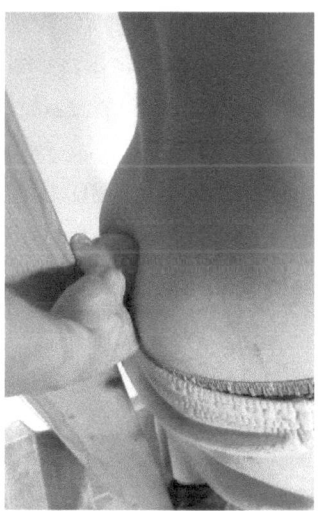 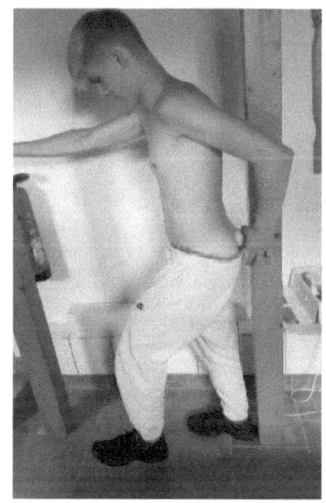

You stand with your buttocks against a frame, hold a tennis ball at the base of the intergluteal folds as described in the pictures and swing with one leg 30 times back and forth, then the other leg 30 times. If there is no ball at hand, you can also press one half of your buttocks against the frame and move one leg back and forth 30 times, then the other leg.

You should change sides 3 times, then you have moved every leg 90 times.

In the morning and evening, move your right leg 90 times and your left leg 90 times. Afterwards you have to correct the hip two or three times as described, because the hip slips out when the leg swings.

If you cannot swing your leg 90 times at the beginning, you should start with 30 swings per leg and spread the exercises over the day. Maybe after one or two hours another 30 times swinging each leg back and forth in the door frame. 90 movements per day should be a minimum to be successful.

During the first 6-8 weeks, one leg should be moved 90 to 180 times a day, then the other leg in the door frame, with or without the ball

The correction is very important because the muscles need approximately 6-8 weeks or even longer to change.

These two exercises can change your life, just start.

I do these exercises every day, I am healthy and have no more pain. As already described, I don't have to take into consideration anything anymore in everyday life. If it should pinch somewhere, I do the exercises more intensively.

I often have to remind my wife of this, because when you feel well, it is easy to forget the exercises. That's how human beings are. And it really doesn't take much time.

I wish you much success.

These exercises are also very important for prevention, before and after every sport, you don't have to get back pain first.

Exercises one and two again described

The two exercises

Hip and leg length correction

The exercise should be done lying on your back or in standing position.

a) standing position

Lift one leg until its thigh is approximately horizontal. Now press your fist against the thigh, as described in the pictures.

Move the leg a little bit outwards and place the leg on the floor again next to the other one in such a way that the foot describes a small arc, just like riding a bicycle, until it is next to the other foot again. This exercise is particularly recommended before and after driving a car and after sitting for a long time. In stubborn cases, do it after each sitting.

Lift one leg until its thigh is approximately horizontal. Now press your fist against the thigh as described in the pictures.

b) Lying on the back

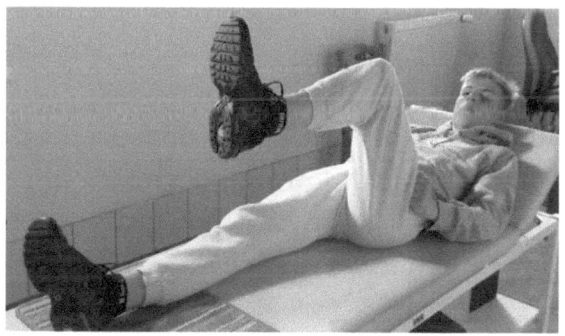

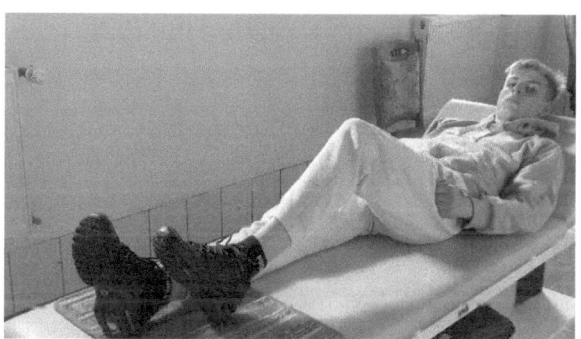

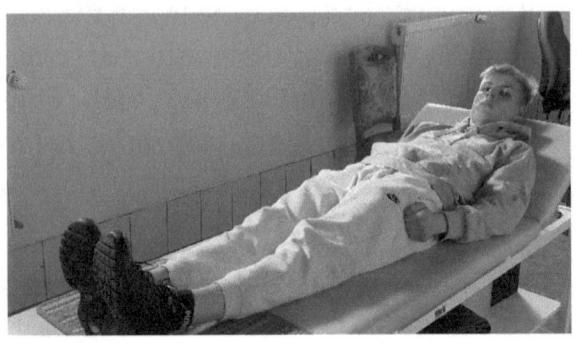

As described in the pictures

The movements when lying are the same as in standing position. You bend one leg until thigh and torso form a right angle. You place your fist against the upper thigh, as in the pictures. But only when the leg is lowered again(fist at the trouser seam, keep arms as long as they are) you press against the thigh, while at the same time you put down the leg with a slight bow movement.

Make sure that you press with your fist against the thigh until the exercise leg is next to the other one.

This exercise is particularly efficient, if carried out daily in bed before going to sleep, because the femoral head is then in the hip socket throughout the night and the ligaments can regenerate. This efficiency is also achieved in the morning before getting up. Since you turn at night, you should also do this exercise in the morning about 4 times right and left alternating (right, left, right, left, right,...).

Sacrum correction

Press one-half of your buttocks against the door frame, with your hands against the other door frame to put some pressure on the sacrum, then start swinging the leg back and forth 30 times.

Then turn around and swing the other leg 30 times back and forth. This exercise should be repeated 3 times so that you have moved your leg 90 times, daily in the morning and evening.

After the exercise (correction of the sacrum) the hip must be corrected as described. First exercise.

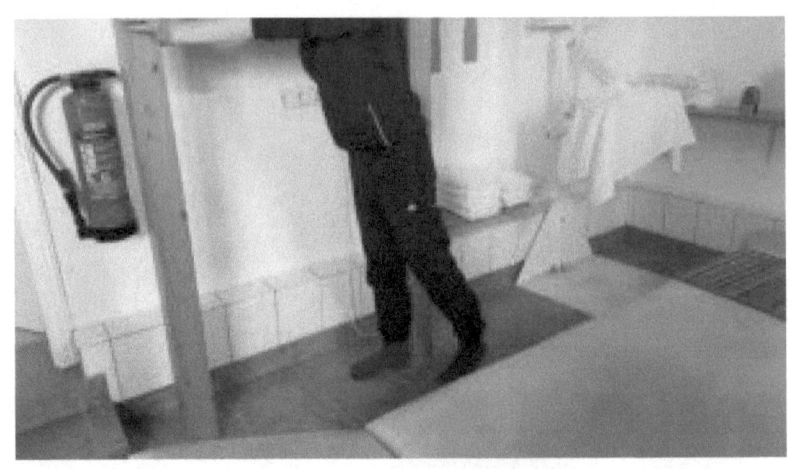

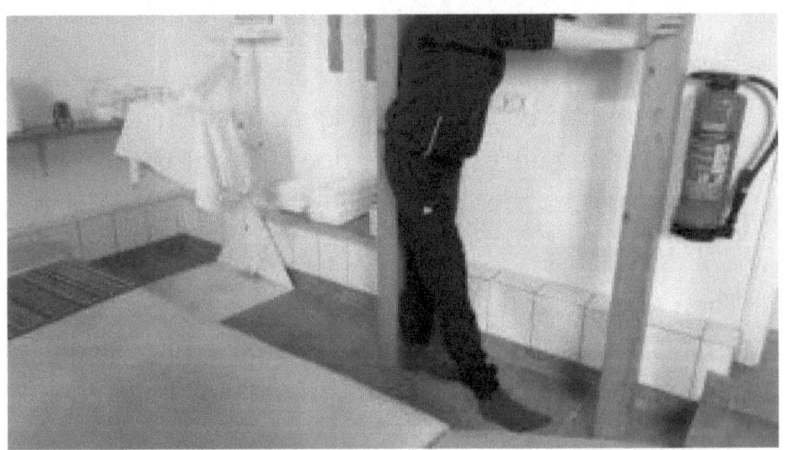

Zeitfracht Medien GmbH
Ferdinand-Jühlke-Straße 7
99095 Erfurt, Deutschland
produktsicherheit@kolibri360.de